WIND, FROST & FIRE

Published by AB collector publishing
215 Sand Point Road, Lakeville Corner
New Brunswick, Canada E4B 1K5
In-house editor Astrid Brunner

Distributed by Impresses/M. Somerville Distributors Ltd.
PO Box 20022, Saint John, New Brunswick, Canada E2L 5B2
Tel 506-642-5514 Fax 506-642-5515
E-mail: info@murderhill.com/impbooks@nb.aibn.com
Web: http://www.murderhill.com

Original cover art by: José Mimó y Mena
Author photograph by: Jacques Bouvard
Book design by Pete Stafford, CP&D
Typeface Berkeley
Printed by Print Atlantic
Manufactured in Canada

National Library of Canada Cataloguing in Publication Data

Bouvard, Marguerite Guzman, 1937-
        Wind, frost & fire

Poems.
ISBN 1-895466-08-3

        I. Title.

PS3552.O837W55 2001   811'.54   C2001-903990-5

*for Sylvia
with love,
Guita*

Wind,
Frost &
Fire

marguerite guzmán bouvard

Poems

collector publishing
new brunswick, canada

ACKNOWLEDGMENTS

The author expresses her gratitude to the editors of the following publications in which these poems first appeared.

Back Road, Amherst Virginia in the SOUTHERN HUMANITIES REVIEW.

Giving Testimony, La Bora, Speaking to the Mountains and In Sarajevo in PRAIRIE SCHOONER.

Above the Mountains, Empire, She Has Become an Older Woman, in QUARTERLY REVIEW OF LITERATURE 50th ANNIVERSARY ANTHOLOGY.

Weaving the Air Between Us, in RADCLIFFE QUARTERLY.

With Giacometti in LITERARY REVIEW.

Father Sky, Mother Earth and Helen Keller in MIDWEST QUARTERLY.

Like the First Peoples in BLOOMSBURY REVIEW.

How It Begins, Second Exile and After the Storm in THE JOURNAL OF KENTUCKY STUDIES.

That Moment, The River in WIND, Happiness in SHENANDOAH.

In My Room and Shattering the Silence in WOMEN'S REVIEW OF BOOKS.

With My Father in Mexico in CONFRONTATION.

Taos Pueblo in AFTERTHOUGHTS.

At San Francisco de Asis in SANTA FE BROADSIDE.

Cover painting by José Mimó y Mena

With grateful acknowledgement to the Virginia Center for the Creative Arts where so many of these poems were written.

TABLE OF CONTENTS

TABLE OF CONTENTS (Cont.)

PART 1

GIVING TESTIMONY

"Don't look," he says, covering the newspaper,
and I remember my mother steering me away
from an accident while we walked
down the street. Matuschka,
they want your disfigurement
to remain invisible. They want you
to be that perfect model's body,
slim, elegant, carved
in alabaster. But you posed
for the front cover with your scar,
the crater where the scalpel gouged
out your breast. "Give it air,"
I tell him, "give it space." The light
never discriminates. Bare your wound,
let its voice instruct us
when we are afraid, telling us
not only of survival and pain, but
of courage and resistance, what it is
to be wounded yet whole.

POEM FOR MAMIE

It's not the mountain with its symphony
of passing clouds, or the cowbells' rhythmic
clang or the birds' shrill twittering
lapping the day like waves
that draws me, but a woman
nailed to her chair by age,
her bones friable as thinned shale.
The house she tended more carefully
than her own children -- starched curtains
muting the sun, doors opening
to a garden she no longer visits --
has the weight and consistency of iron.
She knows how floors creak,
thinking she might have read books,
strayed beyond her husband's
voice, tried to understand her children.
They bustle in from their brimming days
where time flows so swiftly
while she's impaled by the present.
I want to tell her it's not only
the mountain with its procession of clouds,
its scents of newly mown hay, but she
herself, beached in raw dailiness,
is also moving, that a life is more
than the sum of its parts, is the one
poem that is always opening.

THE BOOK OF NIGHTS

1

All night, trucks continue beating
their schedules, sirens advertise
the violence of our lives, and I am pacing inside
a body that no longer recognizes
intervals of light and dark, waiting
for the gentle deliverance of birdsong.

2

"Wise as an owl," we like to say, but owls
are blinded by light. What they know is how to swoop
for the kill, how to read the smallest rustle
in the leaves. They know that daylight
is only a pinprick on night's
swirling ocean, that our dreams
get up and walk around with knives,
our anger splashing graffiti
on the walls of our tidy homes.

3

I know she has been there when I enter a room
with freshly cut flowers, a lace tablecloth
laid out with china. In my dreams, the window
is always open, the curtain is fluttering,
and I am surprised to see the mother
I can no longer touch or speak to, she
who has become a color, an afterglow
in an abandoned house.

4

Just when we thought we had gained a toehold,
we are hurled onto strange
terrain, learn that the pinwheels
of stars are driven by some unseen
force, that luminosity comprises
less than one percent of the universe,
and we are propelled through mysterious
clumpings of black matter. In the dark, we discover
the intricate causeways. We become palpable.

VIGIL

I gather them up at the frontiers
of sleep, lift the children out of newsprint;

the spindly Sudanese baby, a whole country's
famine echoing in his scream.

I stroke his forehead, my hands spill
oranges and bread. On the back pages

where AIDS in South Africa is rendered
in three column inches, I open the door

to the rickety house of a girl
who tended her parents into their deaths.

Relatives have moved in, and treat her
like a servant. I become a tree

standing over that house,
my leaves whispering through walls.

WHAT REMAINS

In a forgotten book, a slip of paper
fell out from a former life. There I was
in a suit, striding down throbbing halls
as if I owned them. I stood at a lectern
delivering words as if they were keys
to the intricate machinery of far off
cities. I inscribed diagrams on the blackboard.
My arms and legs were always
in motion as if they knew where
they were going and why. My blood raced
too, drumming its messages
before so many faces.
I was a conductor of the symphony
of days. Then the room darkened
and with my hands in mid-air, the orchestra
vanished. I was left with a baton
that pointed nowhere. That slip of paper
could belong to another person,
the suit hangs in the attic
as if it were a long forgotten ghost.
I speak a different language
now. I am flying inward studying
another terrain with open pages
on my lap where sun
and clouds inscribe their texts.

LESSONS

Where the slopes open their pages
of light and shadow,
and rocks are jumbled together
like the bones of our past,

the lessons still dangle before me.
I see Miss Durgin leading us
through the foreign country
of Shakespeare, when the dust

on the windowpanes seemed
more eloquent and the minute hands
were weighted down. As I gouged
my name on the desk, Miss Durgin,

her face lit with inexplicable joy,
told us that literature would be there
someday when we needed a window.
In late afternoon, the peaks dissolve

into a luminous smoky blue.
In the mountains, I am scaling
the earth of myself, journeying
through illness.

I'm in Somalia, lying on my side
with a bloated belly,
in Dubrovinik, waiting in line
for water. My body ushers me

to the blood-stained wedding
where I finally marry the world.

LA BORA

In Sistiana, we thought we left everything
behind. The Carso with its bauxite hills,
its fragrant thyme, radiated
white light as if we had entered
a caesura and the moments were drawn out
notes. Gathered together at Sardoč's
for vino nero and čivapciči,
we cousins laughed and talked in three languages.
But we were only a stone's throw
from the border. Suddenly that night,
the Bora came hurtling in, twanging the cables
with its ominous whine, and I lay awake
remembering that other cousin, Dragan
the Croatian soldier, who returned
from Bosnia drinking hard, not speaking.

THEIR LIFE

Her smile opens the day, her black curls
lighting her face. Beside her,
he is tall and gangly,
with solemn blue eyes. Serb
and Muslim, they walk with their arms
entwined the way their people once were
in Sarajevo, held in a tapestry
of minarets and spires, of languages
and neighborhoods woven across centuries.
The newspapers do not mention their names,
but how she with the round, innocent face
and he with the steady eyes walk down the street
and cross the intersection, two
children in love, their life together
a burning flash beneath mortar.

IN SARAJEVO

they eat air, hide in cellars, run
between volleys of gunfire.
They paint pictures on their walls
of things they cannot have; milk,
eggs, butter, an enticing bar
of dark chocolate. The children play ball
among rubble, their ribs sculpting
their taut flesh. They eat air.
A homemade station broadcasts jokes:
"Jesus walks down the street with his cross,
and a man rushes up to him crying,
'where did you get that wood?'
In the confessional, a man
tells the priest, 'I did it with a chicken,'
and the priest answers, 'where did you find
that chicken?'" In this city, they feast
on irony: "Sarajevo
is worse than Auschwitz.
At least they had gas."

SHATTERING THE SILENCE

Like the pulse in my wrist,
the rhythmic thunder of wheels
against rails, tunneling into the night,
staking a claim against the peaceful
houses and pastures. It unwinds through
my dreams like the film I saw as a small child
in 1943: Mr. Emmanuel beating his aged fists
against the walls of his cell, but
my mother never explained. Even
in daylight, the traffic of birds,
children and cars cannot diminish
the rumbling of freight cars.
They grind on relentlessly, like creatures
who have lost their souls, like Descartes'
universe set in motion by a God
who then abandoned it, the ratchets and wheels
journeying through space, an absence
within a silence, the wound from a severed
limb hidden beneath a sleeve,
what my father would never speak of,
the boxcars clattering towards Buchenwald
carrying his brothers to the furnaces.

ARMAND GUILLAUMIN'S BRIDGE

The Bridge over the Marne at Joinville
holds a tapestry of trees,
river, and a train in mid-route,
its banners of smoke
melting into cloud.

Carved in sunlight, it is a mirror
flashing the years of the man
I love. It is wartime
and he is a child again
on a Thursday afternoon

when classes are over
and the children who board
walk in formation under the bridge.
All his dreary Thursdays he trudges there
until the bridge explodes

and enters the history books.
The man smiles in remembrance,
his pain blurring like the train's
black smoke as he studies
the yawn of arches over the Marne.

ROADS

Are those the hills I once tumbled down
for the sheer joy of it? Was it there
you first picked lilacs for me

as we walked down cobbled streets,
that strip of beach where we swam
into each other's lives as simply

as breathing, until your landscape became
mine and I heard the thud of boots
fragmenting your schoolyard, smelled

the fear as German soldiers
rifled your mother's bag?
Was it there, in a France riven

by yet another war, that I froze
by the window as the train
lurched towards Le Havre

and gendarmes fanned out
through the aisles searching
for evaders, and there we embraced

on the gangplank of the S.S. Liberté
crossing the ocean again while the wind
harrowed the road behind us.

MY UNCLE MAURICE

Bandol in the fifties, before the condos
and the parking lots, before asphalt invaded
the countryside. My uncle Maurice
in the long somnolent summer afternoons
sitting under a tree with a stack
of thick books while Suzanne rustled
back and forth with the melon,
the chilled Sauterne, a different wine
for each course. Rich tastes
for a communist, I thought, while my uncle's
blue eyes marched towards the future
laid out in his text. Mornings
I went to market with Suzanne, watched
her sniffing and selecting fruit
like any bourgeoise housewife, except
they weren't married. Marriage was for capitalists.
Back from the country, in Marseille, I strolled
down the Canebière with my dreamy uncle,
sampled the bouillabaisse in the stalls
along the harbor. He took me through
all the museums. Did he have a job,
I wondered, and did he really understand
the Soviets? I didn't ask, but he told me
he once drove all the way to Moscow in his old Citroën.

WHY I REMEMBER YOU

for Guy Muffat

Because of the plowed fields
of your face, your worn sweater,
your blue-green eyes burning
with an anguish no one sees.
Because of the difficult winters,

late springs when there was barely
enough grass for the sheep, yet somehow
you held on. Because you raged
when they entered your fields
without warning and tore out all the pines

to make room for the ski-lifts.
Because you grieve for the sons who gave up
and moved into town. Because
when they rip up the mountain
to make a new road, they're tearing

your flesh. Because you stand alone
before the mayor, the municipal council,
and the rising tide of vacation homes,
trying to hold the line
in your own hands.

SECOND EXILE

Their son came in like a west wind,
doors slamming, papers flying,
although it was January and the air

stung. His old parents hurriedly packed
a few clothes, and then
it was over. Behind them hummed

the kitchen where the man
would sit at his typewriter
each morning, the house

where his wife was queen,
polishing and dusting, repairing
and painting, the furniture

and pictures from France
softening the distance of that
first exile. The old couple was settled

in a retirement home where
they would make new friends,
and there were no driveways to shovel,

or lawns to mow. The son knew
what was best for them.
They would be safe now,

in their small suite, quiet
and obedient, and the family
wouldn't have to worry anymore.

WITH MY FATHER IN MEXICO

A blunt light scalds everything
into somnolence, the mesa
with its mottled greens and golds
reflecting images of my childhood.
I am thirteen again

with my father in Mexico, stunned
by children begging in the streets
at midnight, by men with rifles guarding
the ugly, ornate homes of the rich.
Though he always bent to the children,

my father waved the rest away
as matters of no consequence.
He took me for a drive outside the city,
through endless fields of tequilla
and scrub so I could see the pyramids

with people still clustered around the steps.
See this, see how the Indians return
to their Gods, he gestured. As for the rest!
Now, in a landscape I thought
I had forgotten, in an afternoon which settles

around me like a mythical serpent,
I see with his eyes how this land
where we are strangers
will absorb our flickering passage
as if we were wings quivering in the brush.

WEAVING THE AIR BETWEEN US

My mother is sewing on the couch. She is mending
all the seams we have rent since the last time.
She is so absorbed, she could be anywhere.
She is all hands. I am sitting beside her,

sewing too, but not because my hands are nimble --
It is a way of talking with someone
who doesn't like books or grand speculations.
Soundlessly we weave the air between us

while my daughter who is barely five
curls up on the floor with her toy sewing box,
her embroidery hoop. She is too young to know
about differences and how we try to skirt them,

but understands the force that holds us,
wants to pick up the threads flying
back and forth on that invisible loom.
I remember this now -- my mother long dead,

the threads between the three of us
still taut -- because of the war,
because everyone speaks in absolutes,
death, triumph, prevailing, words

that cannot contain us or heal
the torn webs, and because we are there,
spinning on our axes, the earth still
dreaming, the shadows coiled within the trees.

PART 2

SHE WONDERS

When she visits the Gallo-Roman museum in Auxois,
battle scenes cry out from the walls,
a videotape describes the formations on each side,
the geometry of skirmishes.

    But she wants to know about
the prayers the Gauls wove on their looms,
their pilgrimages to the healing waters of the Seine
where votive figures sprang up like brush.
As she studies the ancient thatched huts,
she imagines men and women quarreling
and lying naked in each other's arms, children
running out to play on the river banks. She sees
a tapestry of villages billow and fray, a summer sun
seeking refuge in the chestnut's thick crown.

Inside the glass cases, Vercingetorix gathers his soldiers
behind the walls of Alésia. Forty thousand legionaires
lay siege with a double layer of trenches
and palisades, keeping reinforcements at bay
and the people locked inside. The story
is one of famine and laying waste, a leader captured
then strangled in the dark recesses
of a Roman prison.

    She thinks of the farms
once nestled like hands throughout the valley.
She wonders, is this the way we are
or the way we were written?

AT MURTEN

Beneath the ripple of vineyards,
the cascades of geraniums
roses and lavender

gracing the freshly scrubbed houses,
hums an ancient battle.
Invisible steps pace the ramparts

circling the town as if the borders
still cried out. Beneath the land's serene brow,
lies another battle, that children

never wander beyond the fields.
At what cost the roofs
pointing skyward, their tiles held fast

by obedience, a grown man
asks his sister. They have met here
to stroll among cobbled streets

and vine drenched walls.
where they speak to each other
as never before, naming

the tumult of their journeys.
Their words rip the tiles off
 their father's roof

until their childhood home
opens its windows
and wings no longer mean sacrifice.

BUI XUAN HUY

Your long, slender fingers
have their own eloquence, your black eyes
burn. We are transparent
beneath your gaze.

Scenes we pass blindly speak
in your camera's eye, a ray of sun
ignites a trombone above
a parade, a beggar looms

in an empty street. You who have lived
through the bitterness of war,
in a country where schoolbooks still bear
the scars of combat, two children

to a book and no door for the classroom,
use your photographs to teach us
how darkness marries light. You show us a child
balanced on her mother's hip,

clutching her shirt as if it held up
the world, the curve of a horse's mane
soaring against his trainer. Quietly,
You tell us the government

is everywhere, sifting the most
ordinary words, that no one wants to learn
how a farmer's hut, the earth scattered
with rusty tools, is beautiful.

POEM FOR NADYA

As if you were caught in mid-sentence,
writing at your desk, or arranging
the dining room for a party,
the silver candelabras, the linen table cloth
you bargained for so fiercely
in that antique shop, you who conjured
grandeur out of thrift. Wait
I cry out, oh wait! You left behind
your laughter, your quick step, the Russian
wind careening through your anglo clip,
the way you pronounced vase as vahse.
And what about your outrage, the thunder
in your blue eyes? And what about those words
waiting to catch fire in a poem?
Who will make such demands of the days?
Who will reweave your alternate stanzas
of grumbling and joy? Oh, wait my friend. You fled
with your skin on a speeding train.
You forgot your laughter, your quick step,
you forgot your books, the angle of sky
through your window. And we never
even reached the platform
where we gather now with only an echo
and voices that have no destination.

THAT MOMENT, THE RIVER

That afternoon you were ten feet tall, high
on beer and laughter. Nothing could stop you
and your friends. That man you called nigger
was a red flag before charging bulls.
Three of you pummeled him to the ground
as if he were clay. Then you tossed him
over the bridge and into the river.
He was nothing. You were that tall.
The next morning you woke with a throbbing
head, never expecting that knock
on the door, the sheriff standing there,
volleying questions. After, without giving
your wife a why or wherefore, you pulled up
stakes, moved out of town to another state.
But time stood still in the corridors
of your life: the arc of that body
over the bridge, the river like a huge throat
swallowing, the afternoon gushing
into your days like your own blood. That moment
rippled around you like deepening
autumn shadows; the splash of a body,
the river's currents racing seaward
dragging you under.

HOW IT BEGINS

He who looks at the honey locust and sees
each leaf fluttering with its own rhythm,
who sees not the "poor" or the "dispossessed,"
but each face writing its own humanity,
is the one who wrote that letter to the President,
saying "no more weapons, no more wars."
This is how beneath the orderly floors
of the building on Pennsylvania Avenue
the basements begin to come alive.
A line is crossed, so fine, the clerks
and section heads pouring over their reports,
the people in the streets hurrying to work
or running errands never see it. This is how the gears
start spinning, the terminals spewing
and receiving messages, the hidden threads
forming a net. This is how the young man
becomes trapped in words like troublemaker
and subversive. This is why the Internal Revenue Service
keeps knocking on his door.
And this is how we lose our faces and become
encoded, me, and you, and you, and you.

EMPIRE

The pages already flutter in the wind,
but the boastful Honorius idles at court.
He doesn't feel the cold gusting from the East,
or see the yellow glare staining

the horizon. He waves his hand
and palaces bloom, church walls shimmer
with unearthly colors. In his dreams,
Alaric the Visigoth keeps breaking camp

and his brother Ataulfus drinks toasts
from a skull. Within the gates,
commerce as usual, the rulers amuse themselves
by watching bears maul prisoners.

As the pages fall like leaves from the weakened
spine, we seed the clouds, unleashing
electronic storms. The president proclaims
that our banners will snap in the wind,

though in his dreams, barbarians
seep through our cities. Behind the walls,
we hang on while the century
darkens and a bear-claw of hunger

tightens its grip. It was only yesterday
that our hot-blooded leader mimicked
Honaria, the empress's daughter
who sent a ring and a letter to Attila the Hun.

ETRUSCAN VASE

A lone survivor among the Roman busts,
an Etruscan vase speaks a language
no one remembers with its lavenders,

its smoky oranges and blues, its elongated
mythical creatures dancing along
the circumference. They disappeared

beneath the Roman heel, while the farmers
were slaughtered, the farms
with their networks of canals

merged into huge estates worked by slaves.
The stories which threaded us to star,
tree, trembling wings,

lie frozen within glass cases
in a museum, scattered
among cities like concrete hives,

where we stride like conquerors
uttering sharp commands, suppressing
the languages for wonder and for dream.

BEIJING SPRING

It's like water and rock,
the water wanting to find

its own shape,
the rocks wanting to tower

above the water. Stern
and implacable, they rise

as the students gather
in waves, releasing

white veils, a fountain of doves
suspended in mid-air.

SAID ON RICE PAPER

His brush strokes dance
over rice paper, opening
the gorges of the Yangtze,
its black- rimmed stones carrying

eons, or summoning plateaus
where women rise in glowing colors.
Chen De Xiang is from Shenzhen
but lived three decades in Inner Mongolia--

"Banished," I conclude, "during
one of the thought reform campaigns."
He worked among rounded tents, where stars
rake the sky, people bow to Allah

and totems, drunks stagger
across settlements. Huge dunes
undulate to swallow massing troops
as black clouds prowl with the faces

of wolves. No repentance here
but a man sitting upright
on a white horse, tiny
against a thundering sky, things that cannot

be said. Chen traces a map of China,
his journeys widen to Tibet. "When?" I ask,
remembering the eighties, the years
of rehabilitation.

He does not answer.
Behind him, a half- finished painting
lights the wall: Lhasa that usually teems
with Chinese Soldiers

rises above hundreds of ghostlike
chanting monks while a giant Buddha
floats over the Citadel, hand
raised in peace.

SPEAKING TO THE MOUNTAINS

i can only watch as you gather the deep blues
of morning   as you rise shadowless
over the fields   i want to speak to you
to ask for your cool distance
and your solidity   i want to ride
time and the weather unbowed
but you who are the clay
of my dreams   remain fathomless   you speak
with the wind and the rain   read the breviary
of the sky   steeped in your meditations
you are   indifferent to   our noisy
and despicable wars   shrug off
our migrations   you cannot hear
the grass   sobbing beneath the wheel

HELEN KELLER

Inside the body is another
body, where cephalopods
nest in the coral of the bones,
angel fish glow with their own
light and silence
has its own voices.
Inside the heart is another
heart, patient as ore sleeping
deep within the earth. The miracle
is how this heart
unfolds, learning of springs
that feed wells and water pumps,
the ancient language of roots
beneath a grove, how a field spins
its web of grasses, beetles and larkspurs
and the air vibrates
long after swans have flown.
The miracle is how this heart
no bigger than a hand feels
the world burgeoning through its fingers.

THE LESSONS OF RAIN

Drops cling to the rail outside my window,
let go and are quietly replaced
like one moment yielding
to another. I remember my father
seated at the table after dinner, spreading
his deck of cards, continuing
his game of solitaire far into the night.
Now that he is gone, I see
that this man who spoke to me only
in what he did or didn't do, left me the lesson
of patience, of one breath following
another. I listen to the rain
tapping out its messages, as if I were climbing
through darkness, hand over hand.

THE FAITH OF THE BODY

if you cannot fly   sometimes   it is enough
to sway   like the rippling
silk   of the ocean   swishing
and turning   in its vastness
yesterday   the wind tore it
to shreds   gulls
teetered and shrieked   their shadows
hurtling   over the sand   yesterday
you didn't know   if it would ever
end   the wind pulling you   by the roots
your body twisting   in its jaws

now   you rise up   within yourself
as if testing   the frame   of a frail
house   at this late hour   you begin
again   as you have   always   done
it is enough   to watch
the ocean   riding   its shoals
soothed   by invisible hands
today   could be   a holy word
if you are able   to utter it
sometimes   it is a way   of flying

WITH GIACOMETTI

I

If we could see inside that burning core
behind the mask, names
wouldn't matter, just that deep look
the way we sometimes gaze at strangers,
or lean over the well
and see our own face among wavering stars.

II

We skirt each other in city squares,
the spaces around us like stilled oceans.
Our gaunt limbs reach out,
our presence burns with the cold
fire of planets.

III

In this mirror, we recognize ourselves,
close as skin, yet distant,
crushed by space. We are fragile
as we stand alone
before the policeman's fist,
facing time, the executioner.

IV

Poised on chariots, we are tiny,
and the wheels are huge.
But we stretch beyond
our height. We devise a taut balance.
Sometimes we sing.

PART 3

HAPPINESS

Mrs. Lois B. Larkin, happiness consultant,
sits next to me at dinner. Her face knows
no seasons, her smile goes on and on
as if she had escaped the knots
of daily life: grouchy husbands, leaky
toilets, pains in the lower back.
She speaks of finding lost objects,
of being guided by "intuitive powers"
while I munch chicken with asparagus,
remembering my lover's tongue
in my mouth. She doesn't know the body,
now turning on a spit of pain,
now offering nectar from the hollow
below the throat. Her fork stays
at attention beside her untouched
plate. "Death," I whisper
in her ear. Mrs. Larkin is ready.
She hands me her card, neon
yellow, spattered with small hearts,
announcing the sale of "laughter products"
and "messages to and from loved ones
and pets who have passed on." Mrs. Larkin
is as radiant as the windows
of a mall, as peaceful as chemical,
weed-free suburban lawns.
She is happiness moving among us.

PILGRIMAGE TO THE LOTUS SHRINE

The afternoon light bronzed the winding
country roads. I could almost touch it as we drove
past strands of sycamores and redbuds,
veils of hanging cherry. Everything
was hushed as if preparing for meditation.

As we arrived, the shrine's glistening dome
soared into view, a giant lotus set
in a clear lake. We could hear
the grass rustling, the gentle syllables
of water spilling in pools.

In the sanctuary where lights
rose like staves and candles
burned in a circle, I felt
the silence throb inside me.

But when the gong rang out for dinner
and we trudged up the hill to the residence,
a loudspeaker intoned:

Attachment is the source
of all unhappiness. We are the keepers
of our destiny, the cause
of all our ills, as for that person Jung,
ha- ha -ha..

I thought of passion between
the sheets and on the page. I wanted to hold
the day in my hands like a hot
juicy mango.

We skipped the chanting
and stopped in a roadside cafe
with its aromas of pizza and fries,
its clatter of forks and knives. God was there
all the time, in the sweet crush
of blueberries on the tongue,
the hand in the hand.

THE TRUE MONARCHS

Imagine the majestic orange cloud
migrating from Boston and Canada
to the mountains of Michoacán in winter,
braving winds and frigid air.
Imagine their palpitating silky
wings as they plummet earthward
and trees burst into flame,
or their tremulous foreplay against the sky.
If at times they founder in a freak storm
in the Mexican forests,
a few survive to startle the air
again with blazing glyphs of orange and black,
to return the way summer always returns
when suddenly they alight
in our garden, poised on a flower
or fluttering at eyelevel where we see a jewel
in motion and might even think
of capturing one as we loom huge
and clumsy before the persistence
and strength of fragility.

SHE HAS BECOME AN OLDER WOMAN

She has come to love the winter when light
falls through the stripped branches
like a torrent, splashing
in all directions. Her flesh

still burns with a thousand
candles, but her body has been whittled
by another's through the years, limb
against limb, gleaming like polished wood.

She loves what's pared
down, and knows that empty hands
keep brimming over from some underground
spring. Her term is set not by length,

but by breadth and fullness,
more than it was, the children
swimming from her thighs,
the table she set over and over

again for so many guests, the text
on the pages overflowing the margins.
Her hands now open deeper furrows, turning
over the earth of herself.

She has become a keyboard echoing
all the movements: grief, joy,
each key finally in motion,
each string quivering.

IN MY ROOM

a cot, a table with blank pages waiting
to be redeemed -- like a hermit's cave
dug into a rocky slope

where prayers mingle with the brambles
and the kudzu, with the compost
of events. The hermit perched

in his Himalayan steepness is ascending
towards wisdom. He invites the demons in
to tame them, serves them tea

at his hearth. With the patience of age,
I learn to leave the door ajar. Fear
takes his place at my table.

Death passes through the walls,
the torturer shares my plate.
But it is love

that comes rampaging in,
smashing the furniture,
sending the tea cups reeling.

BACK ROAD, AMHERST, VIRGINIA

It's like entering time's slow
unfolding, the red oak spreading
its arms in benediction, the daffodils
and lady slippers pronouncing

among the shrubs, and always
the hawk riding the currents above
the fields, tracing his arc of hunger.
Mornings I hear the sharp tap

of hammers against fence posts, fretting
chickens, screen doors slamming, axe
against wood. Afternoons,
the school bus rattles past,

dogs burst through the hedges
claiming the road from passersby.
It's all seamless; trees, clouds, houses,
pastures, and will go down

beneath the bulldozers
and the rough voiced men,
under the rampaging wind,
the rushing of wheels against concrete.

AFTER THE STORM

1

The night where I lay winding and unwinding
the reel in my heart
is over, and this morning the birdsong is a miracle
above the smothered shrubs, the vanished
fields. If it hides the rubble
of our defeat, the ice-warped branches,
as well as the tulips and daffodils, the scents
and colors we wanted to hold -- perhaps
the snow is yet another page on which
to write, a bridge for our tentative words.

2

Grief and illness catch us in the middle
of a sentence, and all our books and bibles
are maps without a landscape. I cannot understand
the deluge of weather, or see a shape
in our story. Then someone I have never met
holds out his hand. He thinks he is the author
of his own intentions, but I could tell him
who he really is, the lantern
in Van Gogh's drawing, a sudden flare
on a darkened road, and then I understand
how moments infinitely small like these
define the sacred thread.

3

The storm smacked this country town with its
shacks
and trailer homes, its quiet farms. We reeled
in the gusts as the snow's pounding surf
reminded us that we are always
in transit, that as we hurtle through
our lives, the joys and griefs keep falling
from our shoulders until we soar
weightless through galactic space.

4

Someone said it was Mother Earth speaking,
the Hopi prophecy unfolding as if
She breathed in her own white light
and breathed us out, expelling the smoke stacks
and toxic dumps, the car parks and the malls,
as if She stunned us with her anger,
and we -- who rush through our days
without stopping to praise her,
who cannot see beyond the skylines of concrete
and steel, who pass the huddled shapes
in doorways and heating vents, invisible
to each other -- will vanish in our tracks.

AT SAN FRANCISCO DE ASIS

In the rectory of San Francisco de Asis,
I join a crowd before a life-size portrait of Christ
standing by the sea of Galilee, beckoning
us with sorrowful eyes. Now I will turn off

the lights, our guide announces, and you will see
the glow around his body and a shadowy cross
rising from his left shoulder. The luminescence
is a mystery. I hear murmurs of assent

but the darkness before me stubbornly
retains its density. I tell her
that neither halo nor cross has appeared.
Your eyes haven't adjusted,

she assures me. Try taking off your glasses.
I return to the church
unenlightened where I sit beneath
heavy log rafters and think

of the missionaries counting souls
gained for the Spanish king
as if casting out nets for God
were a calculation of power.

I think of the pueblo peoples
who sheltered them from Apache
raids, who taught them the mysteries
of humble mud and straw.

TAOS PUEBLO

The people with their cafe-au-lait skin
are beautiful, the younger women's
smooth and silky, the men's burnished.
The women's rounded bodies
flow among the stalls like rivers
smoothing rough stones. As they speak
to each other in Tiwa, I sense
their disdain; they are thinking that
our white skin furrows easily, that we lumber
without grace and that our vision
is narrow, our eyes glued
to their wares. They have placed
"No Entrance" signs before their homes,
before a land still close
to the creation, dazzling and full
of secrets. They believe we are
children who cannot see into the layers
of earth from which they came.
They aim to stem the noise
and confusion, the severing
of their bodies and souls
from scared clay.

FATHER SKY, MOTHER EARTH

The day is etched in quartz, the air cool
and ringing. In that clarity which confounds
the massive peaks move closer, and far below
on the riverbank, an elk lifts his candelabra,
bugling to his rivals, an eerie whistle
ricocheting against rock, echoing
through the forest, as if space
had a voice, and the muscular
blue sky was a body.

*

All I can see is her face,
her huge rounded shoulders
as if embracing. She is coming out
of darkness, her cheeks and forehead,
her red shawl lit from below
by tongues of fire. She is all
lines. She is mute with endurance,
an ancient Indian woman carved in grief.

LIKE THE FIRST PEOPLES

Wrapped in the underwater light of early morning
the pines rise like glowing pillars
spreading their fragrance in the chill air.

Like the first peoples, they draw power
from their memories, wear the dignity
of those who live in the deep roots

of their thoughts, who have studied
the texts of wind, frost and fire.
You will not find them among the babble

of voices in the forum. Their solitude
makes way for others; they stand together
in a nation of equals with space

to reach their own heights. We tear up the road
in our buses and trucks, scrambling
towards yet another horizon

while they wait like the selves we find
at the end of our journey, the eyes,
the green feathers of touch.

ABOVE THE MOUNTAINS

Above the mountains, the clouds are vaster mountains.
In our villages, we are at the bottom
of the sea. It is neither light
nor dark. There are always

many layers. Like the clouds
we surge on, spurred
by the deep yearning to live
without yokes, to scale the heights

of ourselves. We flock together
behind the barricades.
The government has fled to Versailles.
The soldiers of the National Guard

have given us their weapons.
We gather in churches to debate, build
a Commune with our many voices.
Months later, we crumple beneath firing squads.

Herded in prison ships, we steam
to exile. In our citadels
it is light and it is dark.
The clouds billow and set sail.

We eddy around the Bem statue
in Budapest, hoisting our demands
like flags snapping in the wind.
We want to speak our own language.

As we march towards the radio station,
a young woman with blond hair
is shot by security police. She collapses
against a burning car,

a flame that cannot be put out.
The clouds ascend in tiers,
giant peaks streaming past
the charred buildings.

In Tienanmen Square, we rise like wheat
after spring rains. We want
to overflow, to run with the gust
of our thoughts.

The tanks harrow us under.
We leave banners of blood on the pavement.
Above the mountains rise
vaster mountains.

THE WIND AS SPIRIT

Everything swoops upward: the wild anarchy
of pollen, clouds rushing
in distant peaks. The air's
a giant sail, pulling us in its wake,
blurting out its truth;
we are whirling in the spiral
of a sacred dance where
doors bang open towards the light,
a sea of wild shallots inundates
an abandoned field, and even
the ashes rise up to speak.

FRA BARTOLOMEO
SAINT CATHERINE OF SIENNA

She is kneeling in three quarters view,
hands raised before her
like glowing candelabras.
She seems poised for flight, almost to soar
in place in that hushed room
with her veil frothing around her
hurling bolts of energy,
as if she had loosed a current
from an underground spring,
as if she had opened her breast.

FLEURS DES ALPES

for Ariel

Forget iron cliffs, the towers of ice
and snow piercing the clouds. Winter
is over, gives way to the delicate fringes
of Parnassia, a thimble of sky
in the Gentian. At the glacier's
edge, clusters of Dianthus, Selene
and Saxifrage open their rosy throats.
It's the smallest ones
that triumph, the Bavarian Gentian
with its sapphire glow and the softness
of new flesh, Ariel Valeria Calver,
dimples on shoulders only a hand's
width apart, petals from a meteor drawing us
with her magnetic gaze. It's not a question
of dimension, but of where light
chooses to become visible,
what holds the world together.

NIGHT FLIGHT

As if I had slipped from the frail
petals of my body, hovering
outside my life, seeing
through oceanic drifts
of color and light.
I was journeying
in place, I was pure being,
vast as the fields
of corporeal clouds, powerful
like the propellers whirling
through the window, the sweep
of wing, as if I were separate
again, wholly distinct
from the grinding engine
and everyone I love.
Perhaps it was the density
of soul announcing itself,
palpable, without
limits, suddenly this knowing,
when I thought I was
bounded by grief.